ANDREW MOTION

Public Property

faber and faber

First published in 2002
by Faber and Faber Limited
3 Queen Square London WC1N 3AU
Published in the United States by Faber and Faber, Inc.,
an affiliate of Farrar, Straus and Giroux LLC, New York
This paperback edition first published in 2003

Photoset by Wilmaset Ltd, Wirral
Printed in England by Bookmarque Ltd, Croydon

The right of Andrew Motion to be identified as author
of this work has been asserted in accordance with
Section 77 of the Copyright, Designs and Patents Act 1988

A CIP record for this book
is available from the British Library

ISBN 0-571-21859-8

10 9 8 7 6 5 4 3 2 1

'Fine, moving, purposeful ... "The Fox Provides for Himself" ... is Motion at his best, alive to the dance of his own attention, in a quiet celebration of private property and aloofness, animal and spiritual.' Alan Marshall, *Daily Telegraph*

'What is attractive about almost all of the work in this volume and what makes Motion such a sensible choice as Laureate is the unpretentious clarity of expression in virtually every poem, a clarity which does not preclude richness of verbal texture and imagery ... if you enjoy poetry which is recognisably in the tradition of English lyric and narrative verse yet of its own time, get hold of a copy of *Public Property* and I don't think you'll be disappointed.' Vernon Scannell, *Sunday Telegraph*

'Motion explores private domains of feeling to infer the shared humanity of individuals. *Public Proverty* is a levelling book, marking common ground.' Sarah Wardle, *Observer*

'Andrew Motion's *Public Property* reprises the big-occasion pieces by that busiest, most dutiful of Poets Laureate. Yet it is the intimate work that makes his collection outstanding, as he remembers his early life and as he manages, amid profound private sadnesses, to celebrate "the persistence of love".' John Coldstream, *Daily Telegraph*

Andrew Motion was born in 1952 and educated at University College, Oxford. He is the author of eight books of poems, of four biographies, including the authorized life of Philip Larkin, and of critical studies of Larkin and Edward Thomas. He has been the recipient of the John Llewellyn Rhys Prize, the Somerset Maugham Award, the Dylan Thomas Award and the Whitbread Prize for Biography. In 1999, he was appointed the Poet Laureate.

For Jan Dalley, again and always

Acknowledgements

Like most collections, this is in fact a selection; some of the poems I've written since my last book, *Salt Water* (1997), have lived a sufficient life in the places which first published them. For permission to print those included here, thanks are due to the following: the *Critical Quarterly*, *Daily Mail*, *Daily Telegraph*, *Guardian*, *Independent*, *Independent on Sunday*, *The Lady*, *London Review of Books*, *Mail on Sunday*, *Oxford Poetry*, *Tatler*, *Poetry Review*, *Sunday Telegraph*, *Sunday Times*, *The Times*, *Times Literary Supplement*, and *Warcry*.

'The Water Tower' was commissioned by Radio 3 for the Poetry Proms (2000), 'The Norwich School of Painting' by the Castle Museum, Norwich, 'In a Perfect World' by the Trades Union Congress, 'What Is Given' by the Salvation Army, 'No Entry' by the *Today* programme (Radio 4), 'The British Galleries' by the Victoria & Albert Museum, London, and 'The Game' by Childline. 'A Brendel Doodle' was written to celebrate the seventieth birthday of Alfred Brendel; 'Mythology' was commissioned by *The Times* and published on the day of the funeral of Diana, Princess of Wales; 'Picture This' was written to celebrate the one hundredth birthday of HM Queen Elizabeth the Queen Mother, and 'Remember This' to commemorate the death of HM Queen Elizabeth the Queen Mother.

Contents

ONE

A Long Story

1 *A Midnight Walk*

I set my alarm for midnight, and took
a midnight walk. This was years ago,
when I was a child first sent away,
bemused or stupid in unhappiness.

Ludicrously wigged ancestors;
Keats and Hazlitt hot under the collar
in a copy of Haydon's *Christ's Entry*;
the granite judges of Charles I

interrogating a child on a footstool:
all these told me I was off my head
just by the way they looked askance
or scathing in the glum stairwell.

On the other hand, the empty hall
and the furious white atom-storm
I survived with such comfort – these
proved I was able to come and go

as I pleased. So I pressed ahead,
ghosting into a classroom where desks
crouched like boulders in a stream,
and the parching smell of Quink

had stained the air Dark Blue for ever.
The window, where I sat by day
not noticing a thing, revealed itself:
cream frame with greenish chips,

and a handle like a cross between
a spanner and a can-opener. It worked,
and was mysteriously oiled, and that
was that. I slipped out to the world

I knew, where I had never been before.
A gust of wet air made the lawn
enormous, bulging like spilt mercury
which wanted to go wobbling off in other

smaller spills. Left, into the Wilderness?
Or right, towards the Lake? I took the Wild-
erness, plunging through its yew trees
with their oozing, too-soft tassle-berries

(red, but grey like in a negative), my eyes
tight shut, then wide. The bamboo clump
had turned into a vat of clicks and hisses,
eruptions of its single waving stems

too hard to contemplate. The Wellingtonia:
a rubber giant which might send me mad
by taking all the punches I could give,
not feeling them. The gardener's shed

beneath its mesh of sweet-pea tripods,
rakes, witch's brooms, and string lassoos,
was somewhere I would never leave alive.
Where was the clearing I had stood in happily

before? Just here, and now a perfect circle –
moonlight focused in a single blast
exactly onto me, exactly, so the Wilderness
around me melted, and I might have been

a body underwater, waxed and purified,
waiting to wear out whatever held me –
chains, a stone – before I broke the surface
in a cavalcade of weeds and bubbles . . .

After that, the Lake: the stepping-stones
a curved parade of broken paving-slabs
on wobbly brick supports. A small-scale
swamp was sweating round the first,

churned up by people who had jumped
and landed earlier, and lumps of coal
were sunk in it – no, conkers, from the chestnut
overshadowing, their polished skins popped open,

stinking, and the eyes inside pure ivory.
I held my breath, and made my get-away,
clinging to a bulrush clump and wrecking it,
then finding each step coming at an easy pace

just as it should, so with my own eyes down
and seeing nothing but my feet spring smartly
to attention, then divide, I reached the centre
sooner than I thought. I raised my head again.

The house I lived in, which was not my home,
took up the distance — cut-out chimneys
and a cartoon tower. Next, the Wilderness —
from here a pinned-up pelt, and bristling.

Closer still, the lawn, which might be ice.
And all around me, which was everything,
the Lake — its silver rippling into pearl,
its stars skedaddling as the night-

breeze swelled and died.
This was what I wanted, though
I had not guessed it: fragments of the world
in place, yet muddled, and me floating too

between the earth and water. Out of nowhere,
moorhens gave their nervous, metal squarks.
A golden orfe, aged almost white so maybe
I imagined it, rolled over sluggishly

and sank. Neither one of them
could tell that I was here, and did not care.
A water iris with its rumpled purple flag,
and that thing like a giant rhubarb — they

persisted with their own lives just as quietly.
The one thing that had found me out was me –
my footprints jumping step by step across
the stones behind me, skips and scuffles

coming close and clearer with each leap,
so I could see how they were being made
by what I had been then and was not now.
Which meant that I would feel my own hand

tap me on my shoulder soon, and lead me
back across the lake again, the swamp,
the lawn, towards the window – open
just a fraction, as I left it – and so in.

2 *Territorial*

The war ended. My father's war went on
in a Territorial twilight: one-off dances
(which meant scarlet jackets and drainpipes)
and dull drill at week-ends – close by in Colchester,

or further off and more exciting on Dartmoor.
'Yeo-boys' was my mother's word for them,
'Yeo-boys; soldier boys; his boys', half resentful
and half in awe, which in turn meant whenever

I heard the brusque gravel-squirt of his car
swirling home into the yard, I felt the same,
caught between a thrill and a warning.
Live up to him. Think what he went through.

Then the car was hushed and he filled
our whole doorway, waiting for me to go to him –
my father, his uniform smart as a shop manikin's,
the Sam Browne slashing his chest like a sword-cut.

What had I been doing, he wanted to know,
which I see now was fair enough. In those days
it meant: do you deserve the life you've got –
and made me stare beyond him silently

at post-and-rails glimmering outside,
at the deep hay field, at the drowsy fuzz
of elders and other weed-trees by the road,
and feel my head empty. When I came to

we were still in the dark hallway, him
gripping my shoulder now, scanning ahead
for my mother in her kitchen cooking supper
with the light off, appreciating the money saved.

Another time, we would all be away to Dartmoor,
my mother and I sheltering under a tall hedge
and protected — out of the wind —
as well as the posse of sharp uniforms

which haw-hawed and jaw-jawed with her,
and now and again tousled my hair heavily,
telling me one day I too might 'like to have a go
in that' — 'that' being the Armoured Personnel Carrier

which had my invisible father bouncing inside it
as it nipped about on the ochre-green below us,
giving bucks and stumbles when it hit tussocks,
and occasionally firing off rounds of blanks.

I could tell this, because the perky gun-barrel
sometimes coughed a cigarette-smoke breath —
though the bang only reached me seconds later,
and anyway the thing was too like a toy

to be true, or like a film, or a run-together series
of frames in a war comic – the kind I often read,
where I knew how the war ended, but never saw
the end itself, only the same faces fighting on

over the same black ground, where days rushed
forward in jagged frames but always stood still.
It felt like my duty, but how could I hope
to join their story? That was just one question

I could not settle, and there were others as well.
Was I brave? Would the son be less than the father?
What was the father's gift to the son? Recently,
it so happened, a small silver-plated pen-knife

which I loved – practicing miniature bayonetings
and stabbings in our hay-shed, where the bales
were stacked floor-to-roof each late summer,
the top ones whiskered by spiders in the rafters,

the bottom ones squashed. They wore down like soft rocks
as we carted them off one by one to the stables
after mucking-out, and I sliced on with my virgin blade
until in due course the knife slipped from my hand

into a scratchy hay-ravine, its silver winking back
while it vanished, reminding me at once of a horse
my father had told me about, a cavalry horse
with one of his Yeo-boys up top, hauling a gun-

carriage full tilt across a flat patch of Dartmoor,
which one minute was brilliant and flying in glory –
glossy chestnut mare, gleaming green gun-barrel,
spattered but polished carriage, spangling wheels

with their red inside-rims, and the fellow astride
swaying masterfully, reins taut but not too much so –
and the next was catapulting into a bog
hidden for centuries under its furry moss lid,

where skinny-legged birds had landed safely,
nothing else, and which now swallowed horse,
gun, carriage, and last of all man – his wild white eye
the final thing to go, but soon entirely gone.

3 *The Aftermath*

I am a child again, going walkabout by day
for the first time, packing everything I can imagine
to take with me: one cheese sandwich, one tomato,
one Cox's apple, one pack of cards, and one torch.

It is not much, but it is enough. I shall never come
back and I shall drink from a stream. In fact I am
thirsty already, and only half way over the village
green, where the butcher sees me, Mr Wilkinson,

lifting one red arm in his doorway; I can just
make out his blue-striped apron, and imagine
the sawdust with its patterns of coming and going.
He doesn't know I'm off for ever. He thinks

I'm carrying a bag with fruit and bread
for Mrs Reynolds, whose husband died.
Sunlight bores from the hard centre of the sky,
and the butcher melts under his awning –

he is the last thing I see before the main road,
which in those days was not main, and soon
dropped behind me with a meagre lorry-rumble
and quick car-fizz, when what I'd hoped for

was the stupendously huge thunderous passing
of a combine, the tarmac wrinkled by sheer weight,
and a queue of drivers behind wanting to feel angry
but in truth children like me, entertained and patient.

It was that time of year, the aftermath, and when
I scraped over a barred gate on the far side of the road
a field they had already cut was lying entirely open.
I had never been there before, and had never felt

such emptiness under a wide heaven. With hedges
grubbed out, and close-cropped stubble swelling
and sinking for such a blinding distance, and sky
lifted yet at the same time crushing onto me

– with all this, my head was travelling
at ground level, hunting for a sense of balance.
Did I keep moving forward? I did, at a snail's pace,
hauling myself up the speckled crest of a dock-leaf,

then roller-coastering into a rubble of dry earth-crumbs,
ant eggs and wheat husks. Everything was fascinating
but an obstacle, and I had to examine the least detail:
a straw stem, a flint scale, a wormcast like wet ribbon.

How did I miss the spinney, moored there in mid-field?
By keeping my head down, as I say. By not looking
at the larger thing, or what was happening. But these
were real and solid trees which squeezed round me:

satin-skinned beeches; disgruntled oaks;
and a birch with leaves like grease spots.
Everything was as it should be, yet the dead twigs
went so quiet underfoot I might have been on air –

and it was cold, too, though the sun still danced
round the spinney on all sides, sticking in thin pins
and knife-blades, trying to get at me and failing.
I found a fallen tree near the centre, a young ash

with its leaf-hair mussed and threadbare, its root-ball
like a stubbed-out cigarette, and straight away
sat down, dizzy in the fug of mushroom-rot.
A collar dove landed in a flurry, then came back

under control with a display of wing-origami;
a bright orange spider abseiled from the root-stub;
the sun-blades kept up their dare-devil lancing
but missed me by so much, I might not have existed.

I had never planned it, but I felt myself dissolving –
my heart slowing to nothing, my brain running out,
all of me adrift in a mote-dance of dust and spores
and happy, until the sunlight sheathed its blades,

the spinney cooled and blackened, and the duller
silence told me I was hungry and expected home.
The thing I could not see, stumbling through the trees,
across the ditch, and then the stubble-spread, was how

it would still be going on years later, still going on now,
in the long aftermath since I have tried to reach there again,
setting off in secret across the hot village green
with the butcher lifting his red arm, the plastic bag

cumbersome and sticky in my hand, the traffic quiet,
and the enormous field opening before me, in which
there was never a single tree, much less a spinney,
but the whole expanse just clear and flat for ever.

4 *Serenade*

There were the two ponies –
and there was Serenade, which belonged
to my mother. Though 'who belonged'
would be better, in view of the girlish head-lift

she had, and her flounce to and fro in the lumpy field,
and that big womanish rump I always gave a wide berth to.
When the blacksmith came to shoe her, which was seldom
in summer, but otherwise often, she would let him hoist

and stretch out first one hind leg, then the other,
with a definitely melancholy, embarrassed restraint.
The blacksmith was ferret-faced and rat-bodied,
hardly man enough to keep aloft the great weight

of one-foot-at-a-time, though he did keep it sort of
aloft, crouched over double, and bent at the knees,
to make a peculiar angle which held each hoof still
on his battle-scarred apron. He would set up shop

under the covered entrance-way between
our house and the stable block: a ramshackle
clapboard affair, black (or black weathering to green),
with swallows' mud villages proliferating in the rafters.

I liked it there in the drive-through,
which was also where we parked the car (but not
on his days) — for the oil-maps on the dusty cement
brilliant as the wet skin of a trout, and for the puzzling

swallow-shit patterns, and most of all for that place
by the corner drain where a grass-snake had appeared
once, an electric-green, sleepy-looking marvel
which, when it disappeared, left a print of itself

that stayed in the mind for ever. The blacksmith
always did cold shoeing, prising off each thin moon-
crescent, then carving the hoof with a bone-handled,
long-bladed knife. The miracle of no pain!

Serenade gone loose in her skin, her strength
out of her, so she seemed suspended in water,
her hypnotised breathing steady, the smell of piss
and musty hay and ammonia sweat coming off her,

her head dropping down, eyes half closed now,
and me a boy watching the earth-stained sole of her hoof
turning pure white as the blacksmith pared and trimmed,
leaving the nervous diamond of the frog well alone

but showing me, just by looking, how even to touch that,
much worse cut it, would wake her and break the spell
and our two heads with it. Our collie dog sat near
where the snake had been, ravenous black and white,

all ears, sometimes fidgeting her two slim front feet,
glancing away as if about to dash off, then twisting back,
licking her lips and swallowing with a half-whine.
She knew better than to get under anyone's feet,

but when the blacksmith had done with his cutting,
and offered a new shoe, and fiddled it downwards
or sideways, and hammered it with quick hits
which drove the nail-points clean through (but these

could be filed off later, and were) – when this was all
done, he kicked the clippings across the cement
and now it was the collie's turn to show a sad restraint,
taking one delicate piece between her pink lips, ashamed

to be a slave of appetite, and curving away into the yard
to eat it in private. The blacksmith straightened himself,
one hand smoothing the small of his back, the other picking
a few remaining nails from between his own darker lips,

then slapped Serenade on the flank with his red palm,
rousing her from her trance, running his fingers up
her mane and over her ears, giving each a soft tug
and saying 'She'll do', or 'Good lady', or 'There's a girl.'

Whereupon my mother herself appeared to pay him –
their hands met, and touched, and parted,
and something passed between them – and the blacksmith
took off his apron, with its colours of a battered tin bowl,

folded it, and carried it before him in a lordly fashion,
using it as a cushion for his collapsed bag of hammers,
clippers, knives, files, pliers and nails to the van
which he had parked in the lane some distance from us,

while my mother untied the halter and led her horse away.
There was a crisp clip-clop over the stable yard,
and a train of hoof-prints with the neat shoes obvious to me,
who had stayed behind with nothing better to do than look.

This was Serenade, who would later throw my mother
as they jumped out of a wood into sunlight, and who,
taking all possible pains not to trample her down, or even
touch her, was nevertheless the means to an end, which

was death. Now I am as old as my mother was then,
at the time of her fall, and I can see Serenade clearly
in her own later life, poor dumb creature nobody blamed,
or could easily like any more either, which meant nobody

came to talk to her much in the spot she eventually found
under the spiky may tree in the field, and still less
came to shoe her, so her hooves grew long and crinkled
round the edges like wet cardboard (except they were hard)

while she just stood there not knowing what she had done,
or went off with her girlish flounce and conker-coloured arse,
waiting for something important to happen, only nothing
                                        ever did,
beyond the next day and the next, and one thing leading to
                                        another.

The Water Tower

If a drilling-rig clanked inland
and made a stand
in some corner of a barley field –

its elephant legs
and pendulous cable guts
cleaned and bleached and thinned

by the massage of a summer wind
to four stocky struts,
its platform also stripped

to a whitewashed cell
with eyes turned everywhere at once –
if such a thing were possible

or worth imagining,
this water tower would be the best result.
Or maybe it dropped in from outer space.

Or then again maybe
its white and height are really like
a lighthouse that the sea

shrank back from then forgot.
That doesn't matter now.
What does is how,

some forty years ago and recently
arrived to settle hereabouts,
I made this tower the furthest

fixed point of a walk and stood
exactly where I stand today,
four-square inside the circle

of its influence, and thought
these fields of silver-whiskered barley,
dog-rose hedges, gravel lanes,

ash- and beech-tree spinnies
where the muntjak live their nervous lives,
would never seem so nearly

elements which made a grand design
if not for this: incomprehensible
and silent at the heart of things.

Except the silence broke.
It's over there! That's what I heard —
a joke against the ear

as if a bird had spoken, or the air
rubbed hard enough against itself
to squeak — a joke

I put to rest by thinking carefully:
there must be men at work
inside the tower. *It's over there!*

The same words feathered down again,
by which I understood I must be due
for home,

so made my way
immediately along those gravel lanes.
These gravel lanes, I mean –

the same today as then, although
I'm killing time
with just a visit now,

and what was over there
I reached and passed
and moved away from years ago,

and still can't see – as like the wind
parading through the barley
while I leave the shadow of the tower

and finish here
as anything: a single cat's paw
dabbing cautiously one minute,

then a solid blow
which batters down the heads so far
I think they won't recover.

TWO

The Stormcloud of the Nineteenth Century

1 *The Norwich School of Painting*

This long green track
is working its way back
to old England
that does not exist any more.

It starts in all innocence
with an elm stand
and pointless wooden fence
riding that soft knoll

which is the nearest thing
in these parts to a hill,
then slips under a barrel-
vault ceiling of beech leaves

where it is endless evening,
the air thick canvas
so sunlight cannot pass
through except in quick

flinches and flicks,
and the lass and her lover
the shy drover
easily take cover

for the obvious reason.
Bramble banks close in.
Luminous silver moss
draping its furry skin

over dim sandstone rocks
and even branches
now dropped to eye-level,
smother the shocking sound

a footfall makes.
There is no turning round.
It might be darkness ahead,
or maybe a break

and cascading light again –
dust-motes sifting down
like a new idea taking shape
in a completely clear brain.

2 The Dog of the Light Brigade

We have to remember: when Raglan and others
decided their hour had come, and did as they felt,
and ordered their mess-mates and countrymen –
yes, the noble six hundred, most of whom never

had even so much as imagined what shooting
and shelling were like, away from the Shires,
much less endured it – when they had advanced them
up to the mouth of the innocent valley known later

thanks to the Laureate Alfred Lord Tennyson,
thanks be to him, as the Valley of Death, the din
of their bugling and clanking and neighing and stamping
and shouting stretched back to the stables a distance

behind them, and woke there the pampered fox terrier
kept by the men as a mascot, who thinking that this
was the point of his madcap existence, revealed at last,
sprang from his bed among tit-bits of horse-dung,

squeezed through a crack in the ill-hammered planks
of a door, then again through the arms of a boy,
and sped off to join them. This was the dog
who was never surprised in the barracks. Most nights,

indulged with a table-side seat in the mess, he gazed
on the faces of men whose acceptable practice was drink-
ing until one collapsed, whose moustachioed mouths
repeated the same snorting farmyard of noises over and over,

viz: *Frenchmen* and *Russians* and *women* and *Prussians*
and *Turks* and *women,* until they were cancelled,
one by the other, or smudged in the baccy-fug,
wine-fumes and high-collared heat of the moment,

but nothing, no nothing had ever prepared him
for this, for the firecracker racket that rattled
the air they rode into, the po-faced hilarious crash
of men who could empty an armful of bottles

straight off and not bat an eyelid, the curious
antics of horses in kneeling, or slithering sideways,
or stopping stock-still, which is why he kept pace
with them all the way through to the cannon-line

bouncing the heathery turf and yap-yapping
his head off, a maddening brown-and-white blur
at the corner of everyone's eye, and then turning round
when the rest of them also turned round, and skittering

back, bounding higher this time to get clear of the men
he could no longer play with, until losing patience,
and anyway puffed with the effort of running
(although the whole business had lasted fifteen

or so minutes at best), and then strutting off
to the stables to sample the tit-bits of dung
he had saved, before a quick session of mousing,
and after that, falling asleep.

3 A Perfect and Absolute Blank

When friends no longer remembered
the reasons we set forth,
I switched between nanny and tartar,
driving us on north.

Will you imagine a human hand
welded by ice to wood?
And skin when they chip it off?
I don't think you should.

By day the appalling loose beauty
of prowling floes:
lions' heads, dragons, crucifix wrecks,
and a thing like a blown rose.

By night the seething hiss
of killers cruising past –
the silence after each fountain-jet,
and hearts aghast.

Of our journey home and the rest
there is nothing to say.
I have lived and not yet died, that's all.
I have sailed in the Scotia Sea.

4 *Kindly Light*

Pray for the soul
of John Henry Newman
not yet a Cardinal
stuck in the calm
of the Mediterranean
laying his notebook
he always wrote standing
down on a packing-case
crammed full of oranges
en route from Sicily
hell-bent on missing
the heavenly scent of them
so he could conjure up
torrents and moorland
fen-swamps and crag-peaks
lead thou me on
and prove to the doubtful
that some sorts of lying
are ways to the truth

*

I read this story
and made a gap
which held me tight
as a pip in juice
to slither through
then found myself

on the stranger side
in a ghostly grove
of laden trees
where the only sound
was my lifted voice
thrown back to me
as an orange orange
I cast and cast
at the empty sky
for no reward
except to see
how fast it fell
how pointlessly

5 Self Help
For Richard Holmes

I set my course south-east, and go to find
the Margate where John Keats – audacious, well,
and braced to catch the moment that his mind
became itself – hired lodgings like the swell
he never was, just off the central square –
then take the hairline track through wheat fields on
towards the 'clift' (his word) and silence where
he saw Apollo step down from the sun.

I never got there. As I spun my way
through Kent, across the marshes, fog rolled in
so fast and penny-brown I went astray.
A gauzy church came next. Some graves. And then
a man in irons crouching by a stone –
exhausted, bloody-faced, and not alone.

THREE

While I Was Fishing
In memory of Ted Hughes

'Do you want to ...' and sometimes 'Would you like to ...'
my mother sang, never sure which was right.

'Do you want to swing on a star? Carry moonbeams home
in a jar?'

I was six but I knew what she meant. I had these friends,
the Routledge twins: Andrew and Peter. My own two
Christian names, but divided up like that I didn't recognise
them as mine. Andrew was quiet and cautious, Peter quick
and reckless. They lived nearby. You turned out of the village
along a concrete track which ran flat for half a mile under a
splintery ash-canopy, then plunged downhill between giant
clapboard barns, over a brick bridge and – woah! – ended in
a gate overlooking a field with a bull in it.

The day I'm thinking about, Peter led us from the house to
the bridge, and Andrew and I dropped down after him onto
the river-bank. Peter was carrying a jam-jar with a string
round the neck. They were wearing blue boiler-suits, walking
ahead of me in Indian file, all of us as silent as we could be,
but our boots squeaking on the shiny grass.

We reached a place where the bank dipped in a clump of
alder trees. Last year's seed cones were still there like
miniature pincapples, and when we lay flat they pressed
hard into us. The world was shrunken and huge at once:
monstrous ants tetchily going about whatever business we
had disturbed; a loopy spider legging it from blade to blade.
When had I last taken a breath? Not since the bridge, not a
proper one, and I wasn't going to start now.

Peter was working forward on his elbows like a commando

– we all were – hanging his head over the lip of the bank. A crumbling orange cliff, thin alder roots poking out, Peter's hand already in the water, and the blood thundering into our brains. It wasn't a river, really, it was a stream – three/four feet across, with a sandy bottom which made the water look brown even though it was clear. Too narrow for anything, I thought, too small – except there below me, wobbling in the current, was a fish as big as my forearm. 'Chub,' mouthed Andrew, his lips making a soft pop. The way sunlight was falling, I couldn't see Peter's hand in the water any more, but I knew it must be sliding up behind the fish, perhaps even touching him, stroking him so he thought there was no danger.

Then came the trashing hoist and the fish in mid-air – just for a second – the yellow eye glaring, the green-blue body curved inside its crescent of water-drops. Then another second as it straightened and started to fall. Then another second as it slapped into the stream and melted.

In a while, Peter caught some sticklebacks under the bridge, and a Miller's Thumb. Because I had just seen the chub like that – beautiful and by itself in mid-air – I didn't expect them to look much. But they were miraculous. The sticklebacks (three spines not ten) with their medieval spikes and scarlet belly-smudge. The armour-plated Miller's Thumb. Peter filled his jam-jar with water, slid them inside, and gave them to me to take home. Moonbeams home in a jar. No, not moonbeams. Bits of the moon itself, but dark.

*

We were staying at a lodge in the Cairngorms, and walking down to the river in the early morning my mother and I passed the stable where dead stags were hung up by their heels. The door stood half open. Metal buckets shone under their heads, catching the blood-drips. A man was in there, whistling but out of sight.

My mother's dog, however – she'd come along: a second-hand collie called Beauty. Beauty squirted ahead then sidled back grinning as we tramped through a belt of spruce to the river-bank. My mother had forgotten the leash but it didn't matter. We weren't going to catch anything. She was five foot nine, and thin, and often ill, and easily tired. None of that mattered either. It was all in the timing. You see? She paid out her line into the water, letting the current take the fly round forty-five degrees, then began lifting her rod, slowly at first then accelerating, stopping it just above the vertical so the line flew out behind in a dripping skirl, then propelling it forward, light as a cobweb on the river, the fly just short of the far bank, already ferrying through the current. 'You try. You'll soon get the hang of it.' But of course I didn't, not that day. After twenty minutes of picking my fly from the trees behind me, from the grass, stooping over the reel with its spaghetti-fall of tangled line, she took over again.

It's thirty-five years ago, and I've forgotten how the fish took, how soon. I can still see it though, as it began to flag and my mother drew it towards her: one minute clear brown racing water, then a spangle of light-fragments like big fish-scales, then a silver ingot, rigid and heavy, then an iron jaw stuck out. When it found me and the dog looming over the bank, all its energy came back like a thunderbolt, the silver etherising at once, the water empty, my mother cursing.

Which meant another eternity of waiting – but back at the edge of the trees this time, hanging on to the dog by its collar. There were supposed to be golden eagles nearby, and I thought if I concentrated on looking for them, it would soon be over. I searched the sky minutely, the sun coming clear of cloud then slipping away, and eventually breaking into trickles and streams and blotches. The gorgeous taut fish was assembling itself from the broken pieces of the world – gravel, wind, water, sun. It was fixing its bony mind on death, and rising towards me steadily.

*

My friend and I parked in the lee of a barn, already not talking, pulled on our waders in the moonlight, and stomped off through the churned-up gateway as though we could see exactly where we were going.

The Torridge is a beautiful river, running off Exmoor into the sea by Bideford. It was clear enough when we got there – the moon skidding through ragged cloud, a herd of half-visible Friesians frisking at a distance and breathing mightily. My friend climbed in first, and when he had fished downriver for a while I waded in behind. The extraordinary feeling that you're about to get soaked – your skin prickling and lungs empty – but only the waders tightening against you! Thigh-deep here, no more, and the bottom firm when I left the clay-slumps under the bank. And alders plaited together overhead, so casting was difficult. After a few yards and no problems, the universe began to expand and settle. Black water pressing flat against the back of my legs. The Friesians forgetting us and shuffling into a huddle. Bats nipping round a tall ash. Moonlight flickering on the river, on my friend's shoulders ahead of me, on my line sizzling backwards as it drew its sparkling signature then stiffened forward and lay down silently.

It took an hour to fish the beat through – more, since we were dawdling – and after the first few minutes I already knew there was nothing. My friend knew it too. In a few minutes we would find a way along the bank upriver and climb in somewhere else. But while we were here, why didn't we fish it through once more? Just to be sure.

This time I go first. The bats, peeping on their radar. And that sloppy cascade must be the cows. But really everything is the river, its immense slow tonnage bearing down on me. That's not why I am crouching forward, though. It's not even because at this angle I can see my fly slipping in under the low bushes and round the difficult boulders. I am bending close to everything because I think if I keep going like this I might have my vision. I might see all the fish in the river swivelling towards me, all on a collision course but all missing me, like it is when you're driving through snow, and headlights put you at the exact centre of the universe, and each individual flake comes straight for you then goes, comes straight for you then goes.

*

Some time after my mother's death I am reading Aksakov. He is pike fishing at night, on the track of an old mill-monster, and a fire is stoked in the small grate amid-ships. Yellow flame-light pours off the oarsmen and the spearsman. He is, he tells me, in *some sort of half-conscious state, combined (I must admit) with a certain amount of fear.* Later he is *certain that hunters were the first to begin creating the world of myth that exists among all peoples.*

I know what he is saying. He means what happens to my head during the hours alone, with the water making and unmaking itself, with my line flicking ahead and back, with the ripples and little waves opening and closing, giving their glimpse of what I half-see, half-imagine. He means that mood when she is still alive. When the air around me is soft and shimmering. When the mind is intent but easy. When words form out of nowhere. Alder cones and midges and nettle flowers flipping into the water. Glittering shock-rings. The heart ripening in its excitement, entranced, believing the whole of its past has come within reach and is catchable.

*

My father and I went for a week on the River Dee in Scotland. We shared a rod, so when I was in the water he waited on the bank – on the close-cropped grass, with the pine-woods wheezing sleepily behind him. I was fishing a wide elbow, and when I'd been through the bend, and looked back at him, he was closer than before, though I felt he'd been moving away. He was lounging under a green oak tree, the smoke from his cigarette wibbling straight up to heaven.

It was a crisp day, and we were doing what we wanted, but he looked hollow. He was day-dreaming about my mother, dead for twenty years but unfading, today wearing her waders and silver-brown tweed hat with its whiskery band of flies.

I turned back to the river, crouching forward, and the dazzle began streaming at me again. This time it wasn't snow flakes, it was faces. The miniature faces of the dead. Some undulating through the white air, some skimming among the mayflies, some within the water, fighting the current so their hair streamed out behind them, their mouths opened, and their lips pressed thin and white against their teeth. I cast into them again and again, bringing up nothing. Bringing up nothing until a salmon rose in front of me. The whole dark circle of its pool shuddered. Another moment of nothing. Another. But all that time the salmon was quietly gathering itself, sensing something, swinging away from me under the bank so it brushed a fall of bramble, then jinking towards me again just as my fly landed on the spot it had left. When it drew level with me, exactly level, it leaped clean out of the water, shoulder-high. Leaping for pure joy, I thought, my heart lifting. I had it fixed in mid-air, free and separate from everything else in the world, but belonging to me and me alone: the burnished silver back, the strenuous tail spread-eagled, the shocking pale belly and the warrior head. I was a child again, staring into the hard yellow eye. I was as old as my father dreaming in the shade. Then that long second ended and the fish was beyond me, slapping down through the surface and disappearing. Charging on towards the mountains and the stony headwaters.

In a Perfect World

I was walking the Thames path from Richmond
to Westminster, just because I was free
to do so, just for the pleasure of light

sluicing my head, just for the breeze like a hand
tap-tapping the small of my back,
just for the slow and steady dust

fanning on bricks, on cobbles, on squared-off
slab-stones – dust which was marking the time
it takes for a thing to be born, to die,

then to be born again. The puzzled brow
of Westminster filled the distance, ducking
and diving as long parades of tree-clouds

or skinny-ribbed office blocks worked their way
in between. The mouth of the Wandle stuck
its sick tongue out and went. The smoke-scarred walls

of a disused warehouse offered on close
inspection a locked-away world of mica
and flint and cement all hoarding the sun.

I was walking the Thames path east
as though I was water myself – each twist
and turn still bringing me out on the level,

leading me hither and thither but always
back to the hush of my clarified head,
into the chamber where one voice speaking

its mind could fathom what liberty means,
and catch the echo of others which ring
round the lip of the world. Catch and hold.

The buttery sun kept casting its light
on everything equally. The soft breeze
did as it always does, and ushered me on.

What Is Given

Take William Legge, who once upon a time
was forty-three, a barrister, and lived
in comfort with the wife and child he loved,
and didn't care if this might make things tame

since happiness, or what he knew of it,
depended on him working out the place
where everything was most itself, the space
it best belonged in, and preserving that

no matter what, which meant the day
his car slid off a B-road, slowing down
correctly as they travelled out of town
to take a break, and lost its way

at once among short grass and little stones
and ended in the cold arms of an ash
collapsed there years before, which made the crash
hard proof that something out of place was prone

to cause catastrophe, and killed his wife
and child by folding sharply in-
wards on itself, he had no discipline
to settle him, no stable law for life,

just randomness – a chaos like the sight
on cloudless nights of stars with shooting stars
rip-roaring nowhere in particular.
Or are they planes? Or are they satellites?

*

Take William, or Will
as he has become,

stripped of his name
and his safe estate

now the rush of loss
has dumped him down

in the freezing gaps
of doorways and steps

among others the same
all fallen from grace

with rats and foxes
and even those codgers

the stinking badgers
who lost their place

among fields and farms
so went to earth

where passers-by
might sometimes throw

a word or coins,
and later dream

at home and warm
they hear a spine

creak as it curls
against the rain,

or ice-threads snap
when a fuddled head

on its pavement-bed
lifts, then settles back.

*

Take Will again, his swarming poacher's coat
with long, stuffed pockets, hay-bale belt,
and gust of moonlight cold. He's standing there
inside the mantle of the hostel light
strained forward while the nightmen ask him in
but can't be sure. What is this love built up
from faith and charity? Not known to him.
They ask again. He stalls and stamps his boots
so hard star-splinters frazzle the cement –
We only want to know your name, that's all –
and squares himself, hands pushed down deep
to grip those pocket-secrets, then leans close
enough to smell the food and warmth. *My name?*
He lifts his head. *My name is William Legge.*

No Entry

Where the lane curved, and sidled side-
ways as if tricked by a water-burst,
and the fawn gravel dwindled into clay
thinning above a fabulous patchwork
of pressed car bodies buried to make a path,
there was this dense, ivy-covered thorn hedge

I could just see over and into the square
Red Taylor had made home for his one sow –
slumped and massive, fierce but dingy orange
pineapple skin, embarrassing nude quivers
under the touch of flies – snoozing and snorting
her slow days through between litters.

Then NO ENTRY where the gravel wore out.
A wire barricade. The wind's wiry song.
A rank of plump oil barrels and a sign
with Red's higgledy paint-letters trickling
exhausted, puddling thick at their feet.
I trudged home sorry and out of place,

a guilty thing, but another lifetime on
turn back again, to face a drizzling screen
of long fires and longer trench-gashes,
timber and tyre smoke-castles swelling
then crumbling, their black petrol stench
impossible to catch but not to remember.

I am peering over the same thorn hedge,
elbows cushioned on lush pads of ivy-leaf,
and into the square. There is the brown hump
of corrugated iron like a miniature hangar
and dusky hush inside. There is the mud
in stiff crests. There is the slope and farm

with Red cramming his kitchen window
to glare through me and beyond, over his fields
empty under their tall sky, and further still
over the dales and valleys, the chalk plains,
the fells and glens where bright Spring grass
shoots useless under the blind eye of heaven.

A Brendel Doodle

The question *Where's Alfred?*
is best answered
Inside his own head,

which is not to say
he has shied away
from the push and shove of company,

more that the unspendable wealth
of a completed self
requires stealth –

a floating off
from everything apart from love
into a different truth.

Yes, that's where Alfred is:
inward to what is his,
and doing what he does.

Romantic mystery or myth?
I'd suggest both
together and of equal worth,

not (in this case, anyway)
interpretation, with its sashay
of false modesty,

but pure creation –
the living notion
of salubrious elation.

I have heard this, so
I know it must be true.
I mean: a language grew

– a language grows – between the heart
and head, so what convention holds apart
can start

to know its opposite.
That infinitely complex, vital fit.
Unmusic in retreat.

I'll say it once again.
I've heard this. In the listening-lanes
of London halls, and autographing-lines.

And also home in Plush,
in solo competition with the rush
of weather in your Dorset valley-gash,

within that bowl of shoulder-charging hills
where once, with you still
working on indoors, I climbed until

my head broke through the crust
of twilight rust,
and found itself at last

in starlit empty space,
the place
where self meets spirit face to face,

and gets a glimpse of the ideal
and whole
arrangement of the human deal,

sustained aloft
by what could only be the soft
but solid up-drift

of you musicing below,
fixed steady in the ebb and flow
of what has always been and will continue.

Mythology

Earth's axle creaks; the year jolts on; the trees
begin to slip their brittle leaves, their flakes of rust;
and darkness takes the edge off daylight, not
because it wants to – never that. Because it must.

And you? Your life was not your own to keep
or lose. Beside the river, swerving underground,
the future tracked you, snapping at your heels:
Diana, breathless, hunted by your own quick hounds.

Picture This

My dream of your birthday
is more like a wedding –
the August sky
confused with confetti,
no, not with confetti,
with photograph falls
where the steady gaze
of the century's eyes
captures your ages
unguarded or posed.

*

1905

Nobody heard the blackbird chink-chinking
on the level lawn but it was always there
declaiming its birthright; and nobody saw
how lichen blistering the drive had mixed
green and gold in stubborn coats-of-arms
but they clung on. The frame of everything
was Glamis with its battlements and towers,
and you side-saddle on your boxy grey
inside the moment as it froze and held:
your life your own and all the world unknown.

1914

The shutter opens and the world expands.
It's Hawtrey at the Colley for your birthday
but he can't be heard, or not heard
as he wants – outside, along St Martin's Lane,
a people-torrent runs and *will not wait
to get the enemy*. The show goes on.
And then goes on elsewhere, in wards
where nursing changes strangers into brothers
while your real brothers pack their bags
and leave as strangers, or else go for good.

1923

Jazz, New Look, new plunging necklaces
and snap! You're cornered in a studio
where beauty holds its own but loses edge
and makes a soft advertisement for love.
For love which finds its focus as a bride
and keeps its nerve, and sees its way,
then rides the shimmer of its own delight,
returning to the world the gift it gives
in private – tongue-tied tongue set loose,
the head confirming what the heart believes.

1937

In public; chairs into thrones, people
to subjects, and the shudder of transition
rippling through the camera's eye – his sombre face
an effigy as inescapably the crown
is lowered; your face tender with the load

it brings to bear, and what it means to hear
beyond the shooshing satins and the stone
Guernica crumbling, fire in Palestine,
and Germany again – earth groaning
as it shifts its weight and stalls in misery.

1940

THE PALACE BOMBED: then comes the blast
and choking lift that lands you where
you *look East Enders in the face* – not earth
exactly now but roof-spars, mud-in-shreds,
a gluey crater which was once indoors,
and you *like one of us* – or like enough
to make a crowd of wind-frayed kids
and peering mums, the husbands jostling
with the press-men in their burly coats,
all think you are. And thank their lucky stars.

1952

Basalt blackness at his funeral
and basalt stillness: through your veil
the fossil-face of grief, the stricken gaze
which bounces back the flash-lights to their source
but masks a working brain that sees the years
and years ahead the way an acrobat
might see a tightrope and the audience
below: the dizzy space, the camera-pops,
the swaying line between thin air and ground
and every single step borne up by company.

1960

The years wind on, the world and family
develop into colour and due season: winter
poppies, Spring in May, the grassy Ascot drive
half summer greeting, half acknowledgement.
And everything a system made of signs: the marches
past, foundation stones, the plaques and special trees
which prove your life in ours yet make it seem
a secret too – the way a salmon swells in secret
through the currents of a pool you stand beside,
and glances at your fly, and keeps its course.

1997

No changes, on the face of it: the balconies,
the open smile and wave, the garden parties,
and the hats, the hats, the hats, all pictures
in our albums or our heads along with these:
the photos no one took of you –
the grandmother-confessor-friend, the mourner
at divorces and the rest, the worldly watcher
of the world who shows the world no changes
on the face of it: the balconies, the open wave
and smile, the hats, the hats, the hats.

*

My dream of your birthday
is more like a wedding,
the August sky
confused with confetti,
and lit with the flash

of our camera-gaze –
the century's eyes
of homage and duty
which understand best
the persistence of love.

Remember This

I

Think of the failing body now
awake in its final hours although

the fizz and scythe of city wheels,
the pigeon-purrs, the way light steals

across a bedroom wall then goes,
are not the things this body knows,

held in a trance of fading light
before that dies, and gives the sight

of what it means to be set free
from self, from sense, from history.

2

In the swirl of its pool
the home-coming salmon
has no intuition
of anything changed,
just that the silver
cord of its current
is clear water running,
the lid of its sky
light soaking through light,
without any shadows

of faces or lines
to splinter its path,
and pull out of true
the course of its mind.

3

Think of the flower-lit coffin set
in vaulted public space, in state,

so we who never knew you, but
all half-suspect we knew you, wait,

and delve inside our heads, and find
the harsh insistence in our mind

which says we're honouring a time
that simply as a fact of time

could only end, as also must
our own lives turn from dust to dust.

4

In the grip of their season
the sky-scraping trees
continue their business
of plumping up buds
without an idea
of what it might mean
so long as leaves shoot
in the polishing breeze,
so long as leaves fall,

so long as the burden
of sunlight and dark
rolls round its O
without changing its plan
or resting its weight.

5

Think of the standard and its blaze
the tightened focus of our gaze,

as now the coffin glides away
through London's traffic-parted day

and we, who estimate our loss
in ways particular to us,

can start to understand that here
we see our future coming clear –

our selves the same yet also changed,
and questioning, and re-arranged.

6

On the crest of their Downs
with galloping sunlight
the horses in training
know in their bones
nothing but racing,
so all they can manage
today is the beauty
of sprinting and spurting

mud-moons behind them,
the draggle of mufti
wind-burning to silk,
the unbuttoned gasp
of pleasure and longing
at what might be won.

7

Think of the buried body laid
inside its final earthly shade,

in darkness like a solid cloud
where weight and nothing coincide.

in silence which will never break
unless real angels really speak,

while we who wait our turn live on
re-calculating what has gone –

time-tested dignity and pride
and finished work personified.

8

In the eyes of our minds
when the country and cities
turn back to themselves
this history stays:
the four generations
which linked with your life
re-winding their span

to childhood again,
and seeing you stand
at the edge of their days,
where if they so wished
you helped give a shape
to slipstreaming time
with a wave of your hand.

The British Galleries

Take the Great Bed of Ware:
this never fell
through a thousand feet
of blistered air,
shaking its sleepers out
like a leaf-squall.
That's why it's here.

Or the silver-shot gloves
that amorous James
handed to those
who returned his love:
whatever they show
of the heart's harm
is all in the weave.

Or the fat/thin boards
of the dancing floor
in the Norfolks' house:
their vertical hoard
of empty space
is simply that – a clear
vault where silence is stored.

Or the see-through
brittle lily-pad sky
of the Crystal Palace:
here no one threw

a single stone, much less
decided to die.
These prove it. These prove what is true.

The Game

I must tell you this:
there was a boy – Tommy Prentice.
The afternoon I'm thinking about
he stopped me with his shout
of just my first name,
all friendly-like – no blame,
jealousy, resentment or distrust –
telling me I must
come out with him now
and play – he had friends waiting, although
it was me they wanted: without me
the game was no good. OK?
Of course OK. Tommy Prentice
was tall, handsome, cool, use-
ful at fly-half, with slick black hair
fringing his level stare.
And he wanted me? Like I say,
of course it was OK.

We found his friends
where the real garden ends,
or ended, rather, and the wild
began – wild as in where a child
might imagine the worst to lie
hidden in tall grass, in the poked-about eye
of a pond, in the fuzzy shade
a colossal cedar tree made
as it brooded above everything,

its green stratospheres tuned to sing
a thin sphere-music which never ends.

Back to those friends.
I cannot get clear
their names, height, number etc here —
only that none of them gave a sign,
not so much as one single frown
between them, of what was in store —
though maybe that had more
to do with accident than plan.
Maybe (I'm sure if once he began
to explain, Tommy Prentice
would end up saying this)
it was my fault not theirs,
for being lippy, or having fair hair,
or somehow egging them on.

Neither can I say how the game began.
One minute we were standing around
glopping cones into that dead pond,
the next in was World War Two,
the Far East, I was a POW,
and they were the Japanese.
Ridiculous, everyone agrees,
if ever I tell them. Funny, even.
But for a child raised on the idea of heaven
and God firmly installed there ...
You get the idea.
After that it was a rope and me
lashed to the cedar tree,
the puzzled bark (like elephant skin close
up) creasing my face,

my dungaree top yanked to my waist,
and my back bare lest
the Japanese, who now saw
a good chance of winning the war,
found it hard
to get at me under the guard
of thin air with their bamboo canes –
though since they did so again
and again, I should have said
difficulty was not something they had
much on their minds – certainly less
than I did, what with the mess
of blood starting to flip over
such clothes I still had as cover,
what with the tree
bark's now all-consuming (to me)
fascination: the pale fawn skin,
the parched cracks leading the eye in-
side to soft and spice-scented darker wood,
and beyond that the sense I had
of pure blackness, where I might fall
out of myself entirely if I let go at all.

How long did that last?
All I can say is: it went past –
though having stepped so far out
(I mean in) to their work, they were not about
to make it seem like a mistake,
these boys, not something they might take
back, or think I didn't deserve.
They even held their nerve
when a teacher sauntered by,
a man who, noticing the tableau

(six or so boys with canes
and one half-undressed, in pain)
called out 'Everyone there fine?'
and made do with 'Right as rain,
Sir. Right as rain'
before he surged quietly away,
thick, rubber-soled shoes making hay
with the grass he trampled as he went.

That's when I understood what it meant
to be as I had become:
dumb-
struck, my voice whipped down the scale
from speech to whisper, to whimper, to wail,
to nothing, as my spirit also sank
away from human into the frank
dependency of a creature
on more powerful natures.
When they eventually let me go
I still did not know
what to say except 'Thank you' –
a mumble, admittedly, but 'Thank you'
all the same –
leaving Tommy Prentice to some new game
under the impassive cedar tree,
tugging the top of my dungarees
gingerly up, my face bearing the mark
of corrugated bark –
fading, but still deep,
as if I had just woken from sleep.

FOUR

In Memory of Mervyn Dalley

1

I was going to quote whoever it was said
It was your last afternoon as yourself.
But in truth that afternoon came weeks ago
and ended in the split second when what
had been the plain page of a newspaper,
an absolutely ordinary gin, a collar dove
doing its bobbing-head routine and purr-purr
on a gable-end you had stopped paying attention to

years back, became the final proof of everything
you were and now could never be again –
relics which stayed as you were carried off
all made astonishing by that: those pages
blinding as the air revived and read them clumsily,
your glass absorbing sunlight and the bird the shade.

2

That bright day,
your last day,
a breeze
visible in no other trees
found within its reach
the copper beech
flourishing beneath your room
and, bustling through to its interior gloom,

hurried the whole thing inside out:
each one of its crinkled brown fossil-flakes
which had always hoarded the light
now put to rout,
and what was sleeping suddenly shaken wide awake –
lime green wax-eyes without the gift of sight.

3

I found an inconspicuous place
on the sun-struck terrace
between your room and the beech tree
but then heard your Liza and my Jani
indoors beside you, saying good-bye.
Shush, my darling; shush. Don't cry.

I fixed on the pavement-slabs at my feet and saw
their lichen-flowers – ant-red, pea-green –
appear and disappear. More like an ocean floor,
I thought, than what I'd seen
in fact. Or bugs beneath a microscope,
except they never move. Or dry
tears stuck for ever in their shatter-shape.
Shush, my darling; shush. Don't cry.

4

The long row of a life well-lived: the Sutton
paradox, to start with: engineer-to-be
marauding moon-struck fields (now runways); then
Cambridge and the quicker rush of sister-mysteries:
head/heart, art or science, looking outwards to
the world, or in ... all reconciled in one long drive

(remember? no, not now you don't, but I do)
down through France and Italy till you arrived

exactly where you wanted: Rome – your clever head
stuffed full of bridges, angles, elevations, planes,
and paint as well – paint, music, sculpture, poetry.
Not bad, but just a start. Then God said
(someone said): a false start, actually. Your entertain-
ment for the next six years? An engine room. The war at sea.

5

But pause it there. Your ship, the *Hawkins* – now
its photo's on your facing wall: still riding high
although colossal waves are burying its prow,
confusing earth with heaven, sea with sky.
Your verdict? *No heroics. Wasted years, that's
all. Just wasted years.* Which might explain
why, afterwards, you chose to throw your hat
in with those oilmen (Oklahoma, then Iran):

new worlds, new money, new inventions, new –
new everything, and most of it a whole day's hike
to find the nearest table-cloth. Yes, sir. The task
of matching labour to reward, of changing one you
for another. And you did it, too. You did it like
tomorrow was the only place to live and worth the risk.

6

You must be asleep now –
the murmurous dusk-flow
of beech-breeze

and cyclamen-bullying bees
is all I can hear on the terrace,
still in my same conspicuous/inconspicuous place.
O yes, and that rattling sigh:
you, trying incredibly hard not to die.

Think of it, though. This exact
spot is the place where you stood
when Jani and I were married –
the day you gave her away. The fact
is: you are the one man I always had to live up to.
Now with each breath I am more and more like you.

7

I let myself see your ghost
beginning to leave its body-host.
that's what the rustling is –
not the trees,
but you as you were:
at home here.

Look at you setting off now
on your evening round, wearing those weak-
kneed cords, that jersey with one elbow
out. The blob of blood on your cheek
is where you walked into an apple branch.
Never again. Tonight your head will go
clean through fruit and bark as you stretch
into the chicken shed for eggs, as you always do.

I went upstairs and saw where you had died:
the skeleton of your dismantled bed;
your Waugh and Wodehouse shelves; your snaps
of Liza and the children (that unfocused one
of me and Jani on your sofa, caught
half-drunk, and half-asleep, and all at sea).
Your last things and your first things gathered in.
The things which make a life then stay behind.

And after that I heaved your window up
to look down on the terrace where I'd sat –
what was it? Only days ago? The pavement slabs
just lay there: hard and flat and grey.
The copper beech swung round its million eyes
and met my gaze, and blinked, and looked away.

In Memory of Elizabeth Dalley

The spring after Mervyn died
you sold the house and left
for the far side of the village –
a squat convenience-cottage
your children all disliked
but you could call your own:

a garage-cum-deep-freeze;
a garden of dusty herbs
and low-maintenance heather;
and Constable skies behind
above a hedgeless field
weather twirled round and round

whacking the wheat-heads flat
if it was their turn to show,
or polishing up the clay
to sickly yellow waves
when the tractor blundered in
trailing its cloak of gulls.

Not that you had the chance
to follow a whole year through.
Almost the very day
things you chose to keep
were set in their final place,
and you stepped back to get

the look of life alone –
plumped-up easy chairs
fattened to bear the weight
of leisurely widow-friends;
your view of Southwold beach
sun-sharpened in the porch –

the cancer which had stayed
caged up in Mervyn's life
burst through its brittle bars
and that was suddenly that:
the time you always planned
as a dawdling Indian summer

of soft-skinned cosy days
at home just sitting still,
or watching your rabbit-clan
play their games with age,
or planning a winter cruise
down old Galapagos way,

became the time to die.
Being the girl you had been
seventy years before
and never quite out-grown,
the girl whose soldier Dad
and pursed-up Scottish mother

would sooner have had their teeth
yanked out than shed a tear,
you turned to stare it down
with the slate, unflinching gaze

of the moon in open sky
above an ice-bound sea.

For instance: that autumn day
you ferried yourself to town
and bustled us off to lunch
in the new roof-restaurant
above Trafalgar Square –
where the Gallery's nervous dome

with its coat of feather-tiles
gleams like an osprey's head,
and Nelson at eye-level
perched on his coiled rope
(invisible from the ground)
shouts orders down Whitehall.

You stared without a word,
head turned aside to rest
on the giant picture window,
with a dash of speckled sun
so bright across your face
it seemed you might already

have jumped the life to come,
seen the blaze of heaven,
and knew, which we did not,
that you would never again
set out upon a journey
as long and hard as this.

And after that, the months
spent hunting down a way

to match your dream of peace
with facts as they appeared:
the creature-claw of pain
scratch-scratching in your gut,

lustre in your skin
a bogus bloom of youth,
the squalid incubus
which hollowed out the rooms
and shining halls of you
then crammed them with itself.

To see you turn your hand
towards the simplest thing ...
I mean that winter dusk
you made yourself go through
the kindness-chore of tea:
your sharp formica table

stark with risky cups,
and the willow-patterned bowl
which suddenly flipped its lid
for no reason I could see,
to shatter against the tiles,
and strand us open-mouthed

in an aftermath of sound,
as though we'd heard the earth
accelerate through space,
and felt the silver whoosh
of moon and stars and planets
miraculously close.

I mean the way you found
the knack of how to match
a thought to words to speech
became mysterious.
I mean your hot delay
each morning in your bed

before you chose the clothes
which let you look the same.
I mean the strength to sleep
and then to keep awake.
I mean that strength run down
until each narrow day

had room for one thing less:
your pen a ton of steel,
the pages of a paper
slabs you could not lift,
the weakest sun too bright
to contemplate on us

who waited and who watched.
Watched, and saw the air
you left for us to breathe
grow solid, then like water
close above your head,
and your life slip out of reach

to tumble through those currents
where in time the world
wears down to simple rock,

then boulders, pebbles, stones,
then grains of shrinking sand,
then nothing we can see.

The Message

In Memory of Sarah Raphael

I

A crystal mid-winter Saturday dawn
and the names of things the same

as things themselves: flash-over frost
sealing my garden square; the ash tree

perfectly matched by its ghost in mist;
unshakeable hush through the street.

I take it all in as I climb the stairs
to my room, completely at home

yet free as a bubble in water,
wanting for nothing except

the handful of cash and jacket I need
before I go out to the world.

And here on my desk is the toad-head
jewel in my telephone winking.

Why should I answer it now? This moment
is mine. But I do. I answer it feeling

the terror which started inside me
a lifetime ago, and that's how I hear

you are dead. The peaceable street;
the ash in its trance; the frost:

these all look exactly the same. What's new
is the crash of them splitting apart from their names.

Not you, Sarah. Not you.

2

I rang your number
and heard your voice
on the answerphone –
un-deliberate grace

in a message-rush,
and your hasty fall
on the word *good-bye,*
though you were well

when you set it down,
and never knew
how it might endure,
outliving you

like the travelling light
of a snuffed-out star
spearheaded to meet
the ignorant stare

of us below,
who blink and look,
and are not sure
which things to take

in our little mist
of breath-by-breath
as signs of life
and which of death.

3

In your telephone
the tape has been changed, and now the glib machine
remembers only a new regime.

In your desk
a tidy number of unopened letters lie
bearing your name and the brand of missing days.

In your studio
the bubble-cartoons of all your brilliant ideas
have reached the ceiling, and stuck, and will not stir.

In your children's room
the spine of a favourite book is aching to bend
open, and let the story end.

After Nature and So On
In Memory of W. G. Sebald

Dear Max,
it would be so like you still to be here

twinkling behind your sad specs,
smoothing your sleek walrus down

to bring *a diminution of disorder*
after a whole morning of listening

to questions no one on earth can answer.
But then you were always a past-

master at taking the weight,
and later, knowing the best response

must be *to arm ourselves with patience,*
sliding away to worry it through and over.

I see you now just as you are for ever –
out of the wreckage and off once more,

footing the stop-start quick white line
which holds two halves of the road apart

and joins them together, until such time
as you turn again and abide my questions.

On the Island

The intricate and lovely yacht we saw
was due to go,
that last night lay far out
and caught the sunset like a silver seed,

today has gone indeed
and left the skyline bare without a doubt,
except to show
we cannot think it saw us any more.

A Wall

I have forgotten whatever
it was I wanted to say,
also the way I wanted
to say it. Form and music.

I should just look at the things
that are, and fix myself
to the earth. This wall,
facing me over the street,

smooth as a shaven chin
but pocked with holes
that scaffolders left,
and flicked with an over-

flow flag. Which still
leaves pigeon-shit,
rain-streaks, washing.
Or maybe it's really

a board where tiny
singing meteors strike?
I rest my case. I rest
my case and cannot imagine

hunger greater than this.
For marks.
For messages sent by hand.
For signs of life.

Diving

The moment I tire
of difficult sand-grains
and giddy pebbles,
I roll with the punch
of a shrivelling wave
and am cosmonaut

out past the fringe
of a basalt ledge
in a moony sea-hall
spun beyond blue.
Faint but definite
heat of the universe

flutters my skin,
quick fish apply
as something to love
what with their heads
of unworldly gold,
plankton I push

an easy way through
would be dust or dew
in the world behind
if that mattered at all,
which is no longer true,
with its faces and cries.

Two Eagles

For the sake of an argument
(it's one I've had ever since
I died and was sent
back to live), just suppose

body manufactured soul –
something concealed
yet self-sufficient and whole,
made by the blows time gives

to human hope, and by hope
itself, as it hangs in there,
and finds its resilient shape
in the stream of things continuing.

I do just suppose.
Or rather, I did that big day
we drove inland, rose
four thousand feet in an hour,

and touched our heads on the lid
of the visible world: a sun-smashed
scrap of cloud which slid
off into nothing at once,

and left the way clear
for one of those marvelling views
which brings our history near –
that dribble of talc: our road,

that regular dark green stitch:
olive groves; there, that pink/
grey flash: a tilted-up patch
of granite, catching the light.

And when this was done
a something else none of us
had in our plan:
two golden eagles surprised

from their ledge at our feet,
two flakes of fires, struck out
with a double wing-beat –
over the valley, first,

then over our heads, so their eyes
met ours with the flat
expressionless look in the eyes
of faces on coins. With that,

they tilted their wingtips up,
climbing straight to the sun,
and our mortal remains sank away
as they let the thought of us drop.

The Ash Tree

The perfect stranger my son Luke saw
lurking around our jumbled garden-end
is a good reason to call the law
these days, when the question of friend

or foe is no longer exactly clear.
But the moment Luke gets his finger
down on the third 9, ready to hear
Which service?, the stranger just linger-

ing dips, rises, and changes into a man
with a mission, swinging his Black
& Decker from nowhere, ripping the engine,
then haughtily stamping a nettle-bank back

to get at the hefty, elephant-grey,
cement-hard, ivied trunk of an ash.
We have forgotten. Today is the day
this miserable tree, with its sick rash

of liver-spot-lumps on such leaves
as slid out last Spring, its bare
branch-ends, its boiled crown we've
always hated, is due to give way to air.

We've booked it. It's paid for. And here
now is the man in question: the one
none of us want to go anywhere near
as he slices a hole in the sky, then brings it down.

They want to feel the change,
Luke and the whole family.
It's predictable. This thing

which gives them certain shape
and shade has simply gone.
That's why they come to stand

beside me in the debris,
even though the sun has set.
It's all predictable. We tip

our heads like dolls in unison
and stare. The stars emerge,
bleached out by city-light.

A plane. A pinkish cloud.
It's all predictable. Then comes
that flouncing thump – the echo

of the ash tree as it goes on
falling to and fro between
the heavens and ourselves.

That's not predictable.

*

The time comes for my son to sleep
in his high room where the light burns
all night, and the door is jammed to keep
a clear line dividing him from harm,

and I am free to stay
outside, drifting through this space
and almost weightless, finding out the way
nothing can become as much a place

as something. Now, where once
the ash would fill me with its ivy-weaves
and glimmerings, its hush, its silver-dance,
and seem enough, I half-believe

its murmurings were speaking more of life
beyond it than they were
of life itself. Beyond the stars too, though
I have them in my sights at last. And further

off, beyond the planets with their ruby rings,
where silences no longer mean
what silences mean here. Beyond the things
I don't have names for yet, where unseen

unimagined distances expand – like fields
of wheat in darkness; like the mad
and blackened water only sailed
by ghost-ships; like the face of God.

Buddleia

Travelling by various ingenious routes,
sometimes in the cargo-hold of a swallow,
at others bedded on the lint of a coat pocket

or stuck in the sole of a seasoned traveller,
buddleia has worked its way into this tight
corner of my garden. There is no way

it can speak a word in my own language,
but this does not matter a damn to me.
I have already learned how to cherish

its different ways of getting in touch,
which range from a hard scratching
through to hushed water-murmurs.

Most of all I love the beauty
of its straight-up flower-prongs:
tongues to some, but in truth

like a chemical fire the second
it flares and takes hold. Flame-jets
at once solid and see-through,

a rush of heat, and the certain idea
that what has started now cannot stop
except when it lies low, and then re-kindles.

A Glass of Wine

Exactly as the setting sun
clips the heel of the garden,

exactly as a pigeon
roosting tries to sing
and ends up moaning,

exactly as the ping
of someone's automatic carlock
dies into a flock
of tiny echo aftershocks,

a shapely hand of cloud
emerges from the crowd
of airy nothings that the wind allowed
to tumble over us all day
and points the way

towards its own decay,
but not before
a final sunlight-shudder pours
away across our garden floor

so steadily, so slow,
it shows you everything you need to know
about this glass I'm holding out to you,

its white, unblinking eye
enough to bear the whole weight of the sky.

The Fox Provides for Himself

It could have been an afternoon at the end of our lives:
the children gone, the house quiet, and time our own.
Without a word, we stalled at a window looking down.

Weak winter sunlight sank through the beech tree next door,
skimming the top of our dividing wall, spilling a primrose
                                                    stain
surprisingly far into our own patch. Earlier that same year

we had laid new grass, and the squares of earth underneath
                                                    it all
still showed like the pavement of an abandoned town,
though the grass itself had done well, and from that angle

looked white as the breeze admired it, while we simply
went on standing there, holding hands now, trying to drown
the faint dynamo hum of London and lift off into nowhere.

Maybe we did drift a little. At any rate, something changed:
a shadow worked itself loose at the edge of our world.
Not a shadow. A fox. We saw it droop over the neighbouring
                                                    wall

and step – using the sun as a plank of solid wood –
down through the air until, landing on all fours, it rolled
sideways (this was no stumble) and stretched out owning the
                                                    place.

Big for a fox, I thought, but said nothing, holding my breath,
the sun burning so far into his coat each bristle stood
distinct, ginger everywhere but in fact red rising through brown

to black to grey at the tip, like bare plant-stalks dying
towards the light, but of course soft, so I knew my hand
would come away warm if I touched and smelling of garlic.

First he lay there checking the silent earth with one ear,
but soon the music started and he was up – a puppet
living a secret life, stiff-spined but getting the hang of it,

imitating all that he had seen real foxes do and not been able,
examining leaves, staring out flowers, then deciding to stop
                                                    that,
there was no danger here, only pleasure, and to prove it he
                                                    must

fold his dainty front paws, stick his ramrod brush in the air,
angle his plough-shaped mask to the grass, keep his back legs
normal, and shunt himself slowly forward inch by inch,

left cheek, then right, then left, then right again,
smearing his mouth so far open I saw the pegs
of his teeth, the pink inside the gums flecked with black,

before he tired of that too, and found under our laurel bush
the children's football, a sorry pink and blue punctured thing
which must be killed now, *now,* and in one particular way –

by flicking it sharply into the air and, as it fell,
butting it almost too far to reach but hoiking it back
on invisible string, bringing death down in a frenzy

of grins and delirious yaps. After that – silence again.
When I returned to myself the fox was upright,
his coat convulsed in an all-over shrug

as if it were new and not fitting, like a dog when it jumps
out of water and stands legs braced in a halo of dew,
before trotting off in a hurry once more, which soon he did,

back to the neighbour's wall, and as he leaped he seemed
to hang on the bricks – slackened, to show his skeleton must
have somehow slipped from his body, or so I thought,

watching the breeze re-open his fur, and waiting to see how
he dropped – hardly a fox now, more like a trickle of rust –
my hand still holding your hand as he went, then letting go.

Star-gazing

My darling heart, that night we lay
on blood-red, rough-faced tiles the day

had left imprinted with a heat
so deep but delicately sweet

they felt like living human skin,
we found a way back through and in

(as if a time-door stood ajar)
to how we came to where we are –

the constellations of bad lies
diminished by unbroken ties

of love and gentleness and hope.
The sky-lens, like a telescope

turned back to front, showed everything
in brilliant miniature, each ring

or cross or twisted stick of stars
close-up but infinitely far,

their ancient names at once precise
and wishful, or just meaningless.

Remember? Yes, of course you do –
which means that you remember too

the meteor with its fizzing tail
whose only future was to fail,

yet seeming in its dying dive
to leave the heavens more alive.